About Starters Stories

This new range of books offers a stimulating selection of fiction for young readers to tackle themselves. The language is graded into three reading levels — red, blue, and green. The stories are accompanied by colorful and lively illustrations.

The topic dealt with in each STORY is expanded upon in an accompanying STARTERS FACTS book, which provides a valuable source of information and topic-based activities.

Linked to **The Birds from Africa** is an informative FACTS book called **Birds.**

Reading Consultants

Betty Root, Tutor-in-charge, Center for the Teaching of Reading, University of Reading.

Geoffrey Ivimey, Senior Lecturer in Child Development, University of London Institute of Education.

The Birds from Africa

by
Clive King

illustrated by
Diana Groves

Starters Stories · Red 2

Una came from Africa.
Now she lives in England.
The cold winter made her ill,
so she had to lie in bed all day.

2

Una looked out of the window.
She could see the wall and the roof.
The sky was gray.
Sparrows were sitting on the roof.

'What are you looking at, Una?'
her mom asked.
'The birds,' said Una.

4

'Would you like a bird in a cage?'
asked her mom.
'No, thank you,' said Una.
'I don't want anything in a cage.'

Soon it was spring,
but it was still very cold.
One day a bird swooped over the roof.
It had blue-black wings
and a white patch on its back.

'I wonder where that came from?' Una said.
Next day there were two birds.
They hung on to the wall and chattered.

All the next week,
the birds kept coming back.
They were making a dark mark
on the wall.

The mark looked like the letter U.
'U for Una!' she said.
'I wonder what it means.'

It was still cold and rainy.
The birds did not come back
for a long time.
Una was sad and felt ill.

Una had some clay.
She tried to make model birds.
She wished the real ones would come back.

Una woke up one morning.
The birds were chattering.
She pulled back the curtains
and the warm sun shone in.

There they were!
The birds were flying to the wall
and away again.
What were they doing?

The birds were sticking
blobs of mud on the wall.
They were making a nest
out of mud.

Una knelt on the bed.
She opened the window.
She put her clay on the ledge outside.
'Here you are, birds,' she called.
'You can use my clay.'

Una never saw the birds
take any clay,
but the nest grew quickly.

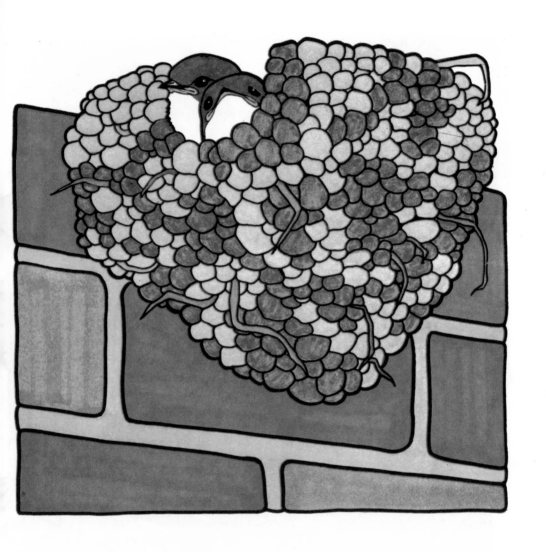

The nest was like a big cup
with a little hole for a door.
In the evening Una could hear
the birds chattering in their nest.

The doctor came to see Una.
He looked out of the window.
'You've got a martin's nest
on the wall,' he said.

'I didn't know they were called martins,'
Una said.
'They keep flying into the nest
with something in their mouths.'

'The martins are feeding their babies,'
the doctor said.
'I hope the babies learn to fly soon.
All the martins fly off to
Africa at the end of the summer.'

20

'Do they really fly as far
as Africa?' Una asked.
'Yes,' said the doctor.
'They all go off together
and come back again next year.'

'You see, the martins
like to eat flies.
Here it gets cold in the winter.
There are not many flies about,
so the martins leave for Africa.'

Una could hear the babies
squeaking in their nest.
'I do hope the babies
will not be left behind,' she said.
'They must learn to fly soon.'

Then — Una saw it happen.
A little face looked out of the nest.
A baby bird with brown feathers
stood in the hole.

The little bird dived
into the air.
Una was scared!
The birds might crash down
onto the path below.

The little martin spread its wings.
It flew off with the big ones.
Two other little martins did the same.
'If you can do that,' said Una,
'I can get out of this bed!'

26

A week or two later
Una could play in the garden again.

A big flock of martins
flew off towards the sun.
Una waved and called to them.
'Goodbye martins! Give my love to Africa!
See you next year.'

Each information book is linked to a story in the new **Starters** program. Both kinds of book are graded into progressive reading levels — red, blue, and green. Titles in the program include:

Starters Facts

RED 1: Going to the Zoo
RED 2: Birds
RED 3: Clowns
RED 4: Going to the Hospital
RED 5: Going to School

BLUE 1: Space Travel
BLUE 2: Cars
BLUE 3: Dinosaurs
BLUE 4: Christmas
BLUE 5: Trains

GREEN 1: Airport
GREEN 2: Moon
GREEN 3: Forts and Castles
GREEN 4: Stars
GREEN 5: Earth

Starters Stories

RED 1: Zoo for Sale
RED 2: The Birds from Africa
RED 3: Sultan's Elephants
RED 4: Rosie's Hospital Story
RED 5: Danny's Class

BLUE 1: The Space Monster
BLUE 2: The Red Racing Car
BLUE 3: The Dinosaur's Footprint
BLUE 4: Palace of Snow
BLUE 5: Mountain Express

GREEN 1: Flight into Danger
GREEN 2: Anna and the Moon Queen
GREEN 3: The Secret Castle
GREEN 4: The Lost Starship
GREEN 5: Nuka's Tale

First published 1980 by
Macdonald Educational Ltd.,
Holywell House,
Worship Street,
London EC2

© Macdonald Educational Ltd. 1980

ISBN 0-382-06496-8
Published in the United States by
Silver Burdett Company
Morristown, New Jersey
1980 Printing

Library of Congress
Catalog Card No. 80-52518

Editor: Philip Steele
Teacher Panel: Susan Alston, Susan Batten, Ann Merriman, Julia Rickell, Gwen Trier
Production: Rosemary Bishop

1 2 3 4 5 6 7 8 9 10—LAU—85 84 83 82 81 80